THIS JOURNAL
BELONGS TO:

_____

_____

_____

WELCOME TO YOUR JOURNEY

Let us capture your essence through the art of writing your stories, your pains, your desires, and your joys. Together, we will create a secret space dedicated to self-discovery and empowerment. As you write, remove any thoughts of self-judgment. Let your words flow freely! Feel your feelings and let your mind run in any direction. As you answer each prompt, immerse yourself in the memories, details, and feelings that arise. Some stories will call an ending, while others may resist closure—too calloused to feel, too painful to accept. Yet through writing, even the deepest pain can transform. Your stories will evolve into powerful narratives of growth and wisdom, gradually shedding their emotional weight.

Journaling is not just a practice but a transformative journey that leads to healing, self-discovery, and growth. It opens the door to discovering the beauty and strength within you. By confronting your pain, expressing your truths, and embracing self-reflection, you'll discover not just resilience and empowerment but also the pathways to joy and inner peace.

Take time to reflect, but when writing, let your pen be your guide. Allow your hands to choose the words, surrendering control to the writing itself. Watch as your past, present, and future merge into one complete story—the story of you. Remember: you are who you were, who you are today, and who you're striving to become. Your past is both shield and sword—it can protect or wound. Trust this process, for within these pages that you are about to write lies the discovery of your true self.

The Five Pillars of Life

Survive - Conquer - Achieve
Surrender- Love

How do you survive, conquer, achieve, or surrender?

Is love at the center of your experiences?

MY STORY

Allow me to share how I have experienced each of these stages in my life.

During my childhood and up until the age of eighteen, survival was my primary focus. Growing up with a mentally unstable father meant navigating through a labyrinth of fears and fragile hopes each day. I had no control over my life, no rights, no choices, no voice. As a child, my spirit was filled with big dreams. But survival taught me to be quiet, observant, and obedient.

At eighteen, I made the bravest decision of my life: to walk away from a broken home without any money or plans, with only some clothes in plastic bags, entering a phase of conquering. Despite the risks and limited options, I chose courage over fear.

As I approached my early twenties, I transitioned into a phase of relentless achieving. Seizing even the slightest opportunities and fueled by those who believed in me, I became unstoppable, fearless of hard work with a singular focus on success. Achieving went well—it always does if that is all we pursue. However, by my late forties, I felt my fears and pains from the past resurface, creeping under my skin, making every attachment—to people, achievements, and even successes—become intoxicating and overwhelming. I found myself spiraling into an existential crisis. I could hardly recognize who I was or what I stood for.

Surrendering became my only path out of insanity. It was through embracing the pain from my past that I found the sensitive girl within me, the broken teenager, the young-driven woman, and the one carrying the weight of all of them.

Through my writing, I connected with the different versions of myself throughout the years, embracing the passion and fire that had always burned within me. Reflecting on my life, I discovered the transformative power of writing.

Today, I continue to experience periods of surviving, conquering, achieving, and surrendering! These moments never stop as life continues, but by acknowledging and embracing them, I build the strength to feel, accept, and move forward in the direction of love. These stages are not necessarily linear; they flow depending on our life circumstances. Surviving a life crisis, conquering a personal battle, achieving goals, or surrendering to the feeling of being in love are all parts of the human journey, regardless of age, economic status, or culture of origin.

Let's journey together to recognize these transformative moments in your life.

Let's shine a light on your own emotional stories.

Part I

SURVIVE

SURVIVE

From the moment of our first breath to the very last, survival is our most primal instinct.

In its essence, survival is an innate skill, often shaped by our upbringing, environments, socioeconomic status, and individual resilience. Our perception of reality also plays a critical role in our approach to survival. Some of us accept our circumstances, while others fight relentlessly to overcome them, making survival a daily battle. Some of us spend most of our lives in survival mode, even without recognizing it. Others may never truly grasp the meaning.

How we survive as children often sets the course for how we survive life's challenges and accomplishments later on.

Prompt 1

Let us go back in time to your earliest memories, as far as
you can remember. How young were you? What do you recall
seeing and feeling?

_____
_____
_____
_____
_____
_____
_____
_____
_____
_____
_____
_____
_____
_____
_____
_____
_____
_____
_____
_____
_____
_____
_____

Prompt 2

When you were a child, was there a special person in your life? Did anyone ever hold your hand to protect you and love you? How were you loved? Who brightened your days?

_____

_____

_____

_____

_____

_____

_____

_____

_____

_____

_____

_____

_____

_____

_____

_____

_____

_____

_____

_____

_____

_____

Prompt 3

Reflect once more on your earliest childhood memories. Did anyone hurt you? Did you ever feel lonely? What were your struggles? Who struggled with you? How did you survive childhood: by being the funniest, the quietest, the perfect one, or the rebel? How did you fight your battles?

_____

_____

_____

_____

_____

_____

_____

_____

_____

_____

_____

_____

_____

_____

_____

_____

_____

_____

_____

_____

_____

_____

Prompt 4

Step into your teenage years. If you are a teenager, write in the present tense. If you have graduated from these special and powerful years, consider how you still hold on to those experiences. What were your dreams? Was life simple or complicated? What brought you joy? What was your happy place, and why? What were your battles? How did you respond to the world? Were you too nice? Too angry? Entitled? Ignored? Terrified? Prideful?

_____

_____

_____

_____

_____

_____

_____

_____

_____

_____

_____

_____

_____

_____

_____

_____

_____

_____

Prompt 5

As a teenager or young adult, what did love, sex, and desire mean to you? What beliefs or experiences have influenced how you approach relationships today?

_____

_____

_____

_____

_____

_____

_____

_____

_____

_____

_____

_____

_____

_____

_____

_____

_____

_____

_____

_____

_____

_____

Part II

CONQUER

CONQUER

To conquer means to have the courage to take risks, fight against obstacles, and take action. We conquer to feel success, but often experience failure, so much that we may stop believing in ourselves. Before we conquer, we need to redefine our own sense of success and remember that inaction can be as powerful as actions at times.

We must reflect deeply before planning our conquering steps: What wisdom lies in the roads not taken? How do we define true success beyond surface achievements? How can we transform our setbacks and regrets into stepping stones towards growth?

Conquering often follows a series of setbacks, highlighting that the journey toward achieving is as crucial as the achievement itself. When we conquer, we achieve; when we achieve, we feel successful. Success should mean life fulfillment.

The concept of success is personal and changes over time. What significance do we attribute to financial wealth, professional recognition, deep personal relationships, individual growth, mental well-being, or contributions to the community? We must conquer in our own direction with our own definition of success while pushing against our self-imposed barriers—challenging both our deepest inner doubts and society's expectations that may conflict with our values.

Let's not allow anyone to sneak into our minds; we should only listen to our deep selves and consider the opinions of only the ones who have proven themselves in the path we want to follow. Tap into your courage, hold it, and never let it go. With courage, fear cannot find a place in your heart. Without it, no conquering will ever happen.

Prompt 6

Courage means staring fear directly in the eyes. It is about action rather than contemplation. It is the only way to liberate ourselves from our own self-imposed limitations. We all possess courage, but how do we use it? Reflect on a time when you used courage to conquer a difficult situation. How did it shape who you are?

_____
_____
_____
_____
_____
_____
_____
_____
_____
_____
_____
_____
_____
_____
_____
_____
_____
_____
_____

Prompt 7

Consider a desire you ignored or suppressed due to
fear. Recall a time when you chose a less challenging path.
How did that decision affect you? Did you still hold the
desire?

_____

_____

_____

_____

_____

_____

_____

_____

_____

_____

_____

_____

_____

_____

_____

_____

_____

_____

_____

Prompt 8

Facing our fears in small, manageable steps is a safe way to conquer desires, test possibilities, and gradually overcome our anxieties. How can you safely expose yourself to your fears? For example, the desire to write a book might begin by sharing short stories with close friends. Or, the need to speak up could start with setting a healthy boundary and defending it with your words.

_____
_____
_____
_____
_____
_____
_____
_____
_____
_____
_____
_____
_____
_____
_____
_____
_____
_____
_____
_____

Prompt 9

Picture a moment when boldness called to you. Whether you leaped or stepped back, write from the heart. What if you had chosen differently? Release yourself from the burden of action taken or from the "what if" and write with fierce honesty. Our unfulfilled actions can shape us in positive ways as much as the things that we do. We learn about ourselves through both our actions and inactions. No regrets! Write with conviction and kindness as you reflect on your actions and inactions.

_____

_____

_____

_____

_____

_____

_____

_____

_____

_____

_____

_____

_____

_____

_____

_____

_____

Prompt 10

Reflect on the ideas of success and failure. What does success mean to you? What about failure? Can you recall when one or many failures set the stage for a later success? Understand that success and failure are not opposites but sequential steps on the same journey. Without failure, success may not follow.

_____
_____
_____
_____
_____
_____
_____
_____
_____
_____
_____
_____
_____
_____
_____
_____
_____
_____
_____

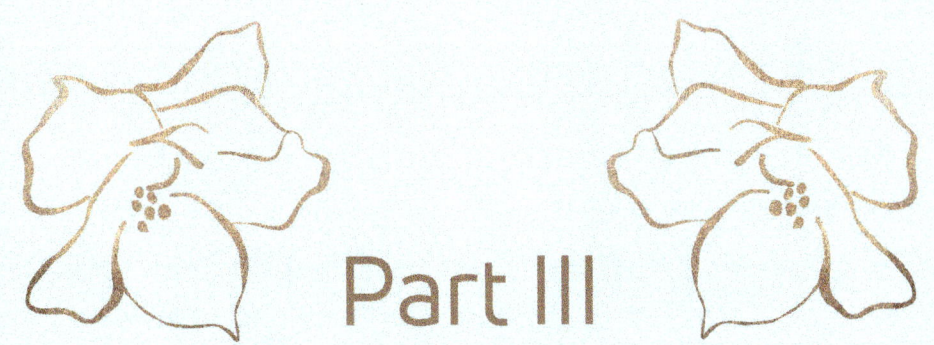

Part III

ACHIEVE

ACHIEVE

A dreamer lives in their imagination, romantically entangled with ideas and fantasies, living as a rockstar within the walls of the mind. A doer actively takes steps to act on these thoughts and desires, transforming dreams into reality. An achiever goes further by relentlessly setting practical goals, developing a plan, and working persistently towards accomplishing them.

Identifying how we achieve in our own lives can bring insight, allowing us to accomplish with purpose and intention. To truly achieve, we must set and overcome challenges, illuminate the path to our own success, embrace the passion in pursuing the unthinkable, and understand that our patterns and actions will ultimately shine a light on our own success.

Prompt 11

Do you see yourself as a dreamer, a doer, or an achiever? What do these roles mean to you, and how have their meanings changed over time? Perhaps you were once a dreamer with love and career aspirations. Maybe now you find yourself obsessively thinking about the love of your life while your career goals take a break. Maybe you take action, fueled by the power of your dreams. Maybe you embrace the changing dynamics of the world, adapting and moving in different directions as opportunities open up, fearless and purposefully without much planning. Or perhaps you plan and execute as an engineer. Remember that the mindsets that defined us yesterday may no longer suit us today. Who are you today, a dreamer, a doer, an achiever, or all of them?

_____

_____

_____

_____

_____

_____

_____

_____

_____

_____

_____

_____

Prompt 12

How do you define purpose? Goals must have a sense of purpose that aligns with our values to lead to meaningful achievements. Such goals can lead us into a spiral, drawing us into a cycle where we rarely feel satisfied but continue to pursue more. Purpose guides what we truly want to achieve, helping us set meaningful goals. Define your purpose by listing the moments in your life that have brought you pure joy, often without external recognition. Once your purpose becomes clear, you can set goals that align with your values and work towards meaningful achievement.

_____

_____

_____

_____

_____

_____

_____

_____

_____

_____

_____

_____

_____

Prompt 13

Achievers often rely on a solid support system. Consider who in your life truly supports your goals while seeing through your values and strengths. Who believes in you? Has anyone surprised you with their high opinion of you? You need them—we all do: they are pillars of our success. Equally important is identifying the naysayers in your life. The ones who discourage your thinking and plans. Write about the people who influence your journey to achieve positively or negatively.

_____
_____
_____
_____
_____
_____
_____
_____
_____
_____
_____
_____
_____
_____
_____
_____
_____
_____

Prompt 14

Achieving can be draining, and sometimes we give up too soon. We may have fears or doubts about our own strength, or we might avoid feeling vulnerable. Have you ever walked away from a dream or a goal too early? Reflect deeply on this question and try to identify the reasons behind it.
 On the other hand, what motivates you to keep going? Do you set specific goals or prefer to go with the flow? How have these approaches worked out for you in the past?

_____

_____

_____

_____

_____

_____

_____

_____

_____

_____

_____

_____

_____

_____

_____

_____

Prompt 15

Write about a time in your life when something incredible and unexpected happened—something you never imagined would come your way. Perhaps you won an award, were accepted into a prestigious program, received a job offer, or heard someone express their love for you. Reflect on how this event made you feel. How did you feel before it happened, and how did it change your life afterward?

_____

_____

_____

_____

_____

_____

_____

_____

_____

_____

_____

_____

_____

_____

_____

_____

_____

_____

_____

_____

Part IV

SURRENDER

SURRENDER

Surrender is perhaps the most powerful yet misunderstood of the five pillars. But what exactly does it mean? Is it about giving up our dreams, accepting the unchangeable, and not advocating for the life we deserve? Is it about submitting to the uncontrollable and letting go of our ambitions? Not quite.

We often associate surrender with giving in or conceding defeat. In a war, surrendering might be the only means to stay alive. There is a fine line between conquering and being slaughtered. But in our emotional lives, where the battles are largely internal, surrendering is not a sign of weakness; it's the pathway out of despair and toward growth and emotional freedom.

True surrender is not about abandoning your aspirations or resigning yourself to circumstances beyond your control. Rather, it's about fully embracing your authentic feelings and acknowledging your internal struggles. This is where writing becomes a powerful tool—allowing us to recognize when we're pushing for the impossible or fighting against our own current.

To surrender means to open yourself completely to your emotions, allowing yourself to feel deeply while showing self-compassion. It's about releasing the need to control every outcome and finding inner peace amidst life's chaos. When we surrender, we accept that we deserve our love above all else. No one can hurt us if we truly love ourselves. If we truly let go and surrender to love.

Prompt 16

Our emotions are the language of our hearts. To truly
surrender, we must hold tight to them, and we must
name and feel them as if our lives depended on them. If we
are angry at ourselves for feeling these emotions, shame or
guilt, we must also be conscious and embrace these.
 The world often tells us to shut down our emotions and to
be logical, but this is like turning off the engine and making a
car run—it simply won't work. The engine gives the power to
the drive in the same way our emotions give us the power to
become authentic, motivate us to live, and embrace our
moments with genuine love.
 Sit down with your journal and listen to your emotions.
Label them, and don't let the pen stop until each word
reflects the emotions themselves. This is the process of
surrender.

_____
_____
_____
_____
_____
_____
_____
_____
_____
_____
_____
_____

Prompt 17

Think back to a time when you pushed yourself so
hard to achieve something or feel a certain way that
you ended up ignoring your emotions. How did this impact
you? Were you aware of what was driving you at the time?
Reflect on the emotions you overlooked, the internal
struggles you faced, and the consequences of not giving
yourself the space to process your feelings.

_____

_____

_____

_____

_____

_____

_____

_____

_____

_____

_____

_____

_____

_____

_____

_____

_____

Prompt 18

Surrendering often marks the beginning of something new. Reflect on a time in your life when you felt a strong emotion and were able to accept it. What did you have to let go of to gain that acceptance? How did embracing your emotions change your reality?

_____

_____

_____

_____

_____

_____

_____

_____

_____

_____

_____

_____

_____

_____

_____

_____

_____

_____

_____

_____

Prompt 19

Consider your fears and strengths: when do you feel most vulnerable, and what drives you to persevere despite challenges?

_____

_____

_____

_____

_____

_____

_____

_____

_____

_____

_____

_____

_____

_____

_____

_____

_____

_____

_____

_____

_____

_____

Part V

LOVE

LOVE

The secret to love is to love ourselves. We often seek validation from others, but the most ever-lasting love is the love we cultivate within. Imagine being your own hero, your own lover—the one who always has your back no matter what.

When you feel down, remember that you can hold your own hand. Every day you can look at yourself in the mirror and love the person that looks back at you. Imagine telling yourself, "I LOVE ME." Those three words have immense power as they can transform you into the most powerful, invincible person.

Self-love is about becoming your best friend. Speak to yourself with kindness, compassion, and patience. This is you, your life, and your story; no one can connect to your heart the way you can. Let go of your attachment to others, as real love starts within. When we attach, we don't love, when we let go, we really love.

Prompt 20

Love, what a profound emotion! Without it, our goals feel
empty. With it, no battle becomes too large to endure.
How can we live with love at the center of our thoughts,
actions and dreams? Reflect on your relationship with love—
where does it show up in your life? Is it limited to romance,
or do you find love in ideas, things, people, moments, or
circumstances?

_____
_____
_____
_____
_____
_____
_____
_____
_____
_____
_____
_____
_____
_____
_____
_____
_____
_____

Prompt 21

Loving ourselves is the highest form of love. How do you know if you truly love yourself? Reflect on the way you talk to yourself in your mind—would you be ashamed to speak to a loved one in the same manner? Do you ever say things to yourself that you wouldn't dare say to those you care about? How do you treat yourself? Do you dedicate time to your wellness? Do you make life choices that respect your body and mind? Do you avoid self-destructive behaviors? Loving yourself takes work and practice. Write down a list of habits you will incorporate into your daily routine to practice self-love.

_____

_____

_____

_____

_____

_____

_____

_____

_____

_____

_____

_____

_____

Prompt 22

How can we quantify love? Reflect on a time when you felt that the love you gave wasn't matched by what you received. Have you ever felt guilty for not being able to return someone else's affection? Consider how love can take different forms and how your expectations of love might shape your relationships.

_____

_____

_____

_____

_____

_____

_____

_____

_____

_____

_____

_____

_____

_____

_____

_____

_____

_____

_____

Prompt 23

Love can be shown in many ways—through words, actions, gestures, or even silence. Think of someone you believe you love more deeply than they love you. Reflect on this relationship and consider how this person actually expresses their love and appreciation for you. Then, go deeper and identify how you express love in your own unique way.

_____
_____
_____
_____
_____
_____
_____
_____
_____
_____
_____
_____
_____
_____
_____
_____
_____
_____

Prompt 24

Think about someone who constantly shows you love more than you can reciprocate. Consider the different ways you are or are not available to this person. List the ways you love and appreciate them.

_____
_____
_____
_____
_____
_____
_____
_____
_____
_____
_____
_____
_____
_____
_____
_____
_____
_____

Congratulations

You have completed a profound journey of reflecting on your own emotional stories, exploring how you survive, conquer, achieve, surrender, and love. With this new understanding of how you navigate life, take a moment to look into your present.

How does this deeper understanding of yourself illuminate your values, dreams, and desires? Consider the authentic, empowered version of you who is ready to embrace a more fulfilling life.

Take a few moments to jot down any final thoughts or conclusions from this journaling experience. How will you survive, conquer, achieve, and surrender, with love at the center?

_____
_____
_____
_____
_____
_____
_____
_____
_____
_____
_____

Acknowledgment

Creating this journal has been a journey filled with great collaboration.

First and foremost, I want to thank Bonnie Salkhi, our talented interior journal designer. Your artistic vision and attention to detail have genuinely brought this journal to life, making it not just a tool for reflection but a beautiful piece to hold and cherish.

A heartfelt thank you to Seta Salkhi, a young, driven, and incredibly detailed woman editor. Your thought-provoking feedback and dedication have gone beyond the role of an editor.

I am fortunate to have shared the writing of this journal companion with my student and teaching assistant, Jason Balayev. His critical and creative mind has been invaluable, enriching this work with his perspective as a young man.

To my book consultant Tristine Rainer, my nieces Olivia and Lola, my colleague and friend Susan, my sisters Carmen and Ana, my mom, my student Laurie, and my friend Trish, thank you for your invaluable insights and honest feedback. Your willingness to engage with the content has helped refine and enhance the journal, making it a more meaningful experience for all our readers.

This journal is a collective achievement. Thank you for helping create something extraordinary.

Visit *TheSilenceOfTheVolcano.com*

Instagram @thesilenceofthevolcano
TikTok @almudenakonrad

www.ingramcontent.com/pod-product-compliance
Lightning Source LLC
Chambersburg PA
CBHW051629120626
46551CB00014B/2007